maia's musings

Mannjiit Kaur

BookLeaf
Publishing

India | USA | UK

Presentation by *BookLeaf Publishing*

Web: www.bookleafpub.com

E-mail: info@bookleafpub.com

ISBN: 9789363317093

First edition 2024

To all my readers, past and present,

Your support and encouragement have been the foundation of my journey. Whether through a fleeting comment on social media or a thoughtful response to a blog post, each interaction has been a source of inspiration and growth. This book is a testament to the shared moments and connections we've built together. Thank you for being a part of this journey, for your patience, and for your unwavering belief in the power of words.

With gratitude,

Mannjiit Kaur

ACKNOWLEDGEMENT

Creating this book has been a journey made possible by the support and encouragement of many wonderful individuals.

To my family and friends, thank you for your unwavering belief in me and for your constant encouragement. Your love and patience have been my greatest source of strength.

To my readers, both long-time followers and new friends, your engagement and feedback have inspired me every step of the way. Your support has been invaluable.

To my mentors and colleagues, your wisdom and guidance have shaped my writing and broadened my perspective. I am deeply grateful for your insights and advice.

Finally, to everyone who has been part of this journey, directly or indirectly, your contributions have made this book a reality. Thank you for being a part of this adventure.

With heartfelt gratitude,
Mannjiit Kaur

PREFACE

There is something about the name Maya that has always fascinated me. So much so, that at some point I seriously considered changing my name to Maya, or rather, its Greek version, Maia.

Maya, in Indian philosophy, represents the intricate dance between illusion and reality. As a name, Maya embodies beauty, grace, and the profound mystery of life. The goddess Maya is often associated with creation, wisdom, and the divine feminine, guiding us to see beyond the illusions of the material world and towards deeper spiritual truths.

On the other hand, the Greek goddess Maia, the eldest of the Pleiades, embodies the gentle yet powerful essence of nurturing and growth. As the goddess of spring and rebirth, she is a symbol of renewal, and the quiet strength found in nature's cycles. Maia's presence is a reminder of the beauty in patience and the transformative power of a slow, deliberate life. Her story inspires us to embrace the natural rhythms of our own journeys, finding healing and wisdom in the process.

In the fast-paced world we inhabit, the essence of healing and the beauty of a slow life often elude us. This collection of writings delves into these themes, offering reflections on the journey of self-discovery and the quiet power of stillness.

The stories and insights within these pages stem from wounds that remain tender, from journeys that are far from complete.

"The Gift" for instance, explores the paradox of a healer's own unhealed wounds, revealing that true healing may lie not in the closure of scars, but in the acceptance and understanding of their perpetual presence. It is a narrative that embraces the ongoing nature of healing, suggesting that perhaps our greatest gift to ourselves and the world is this very realisation.

In "Rituals and Belonging," the transition from imposed practices to personal rituals signifies a profound transformation. It speaks of finding solace in solitude and sanctity in nature, where belonging is redefined—not by societal standards but by an intimate connection with oneself and the natural world.

These writings, or musings as I like to call them, invite you to pause, to sit still, and to reflect. To relate to them in your way and find your own meaning. May they offer you a glimpse of the serene strength found in slowing down and the quiet resilience required to embrace our imperfections.

On Slowing Down

When I slow down, I heal

Slow down
Smell the flowers
Take the longer route back home
Pet the stray, feed it a morsel
Smile at the infant in the stroller
See that patch of grass?
Slide your feet into its green lushness
Stand under that tall tree
Run your palm along the roughness of its bark
Komorebi yourself for a minute
Walk closer to the lawns
Let the sprinklers spray you
Giggle some, and laugh aloud
What have you to lose?
If a stranger smiles, smile back
Let them think you're weird
Rejoice in your weirdness

Who knows?
A few may join you
Know them as your tribe
The happy ones
Who need but little to rejoice.

When I slow down, I heal.
Come, heal with me

Uncharted Territory

There have been days
when Maia has sat alone with her Solitude.
Not minding the space,
enjoying her own company.
And then there have been days
when she has wanted, craved companionship.
She has no complaints.
She's lived it all. And she's loved it all.

Now she's emerging out of her cave.
Adjusting her eyes to the surroundings.
Absorbing it and taking it all in.

As she stretches out the kinks,
she feels a rawness to her movements.
Her muscles move in new ways.
She feels different.

Her mind is conjuring up new adventures.
She's feeling the need to go in a new direction.
She has no maps.
Only a perceived destination.

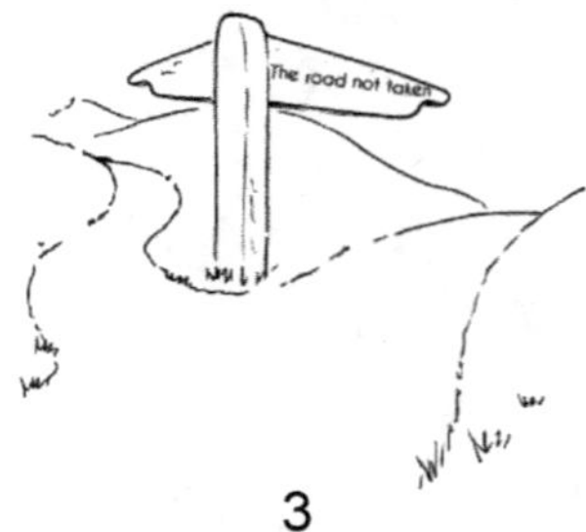

Is she ready to take the risk?
"Will it be worth it," she asks herself.

She's yet to make a choice.

The Gift

Every healer who takes on the task
of healing others is also still wounded.
Her wounds will never truly be healed.
The potion for healing others
comes from her own unhealed wounds.
She takes on this task because she knows
she's been alone and lost on this journey herself.
When she needed someone,
was exactly when she was left alone.
And her wounds were dug deeper into.
It was up to her to tear open the scabs
and journey into the rotting wounds,
to find more of what was still to be healed.

Maia's journey continues.
The path, when she thinks is almost over,
opens up yet again with more to be seen,
more to be held, and more to be healed.

Now while she can continue to go deeper
and deeper, she feels the need to pause.
To sit still and assess what's been healed
and what remains of the damage.
In this pause, she realises
the wound is the same one she began with,
and yet every time she looks at it,

it has something new to present.
Something more to tell her. It seems different.

So now she's asking herself
if there is any point to healing it at all.
Or should she just learn to live with it knowing
that it's her companion through life and beyond?

Or maybe this new perspective
is her true healing.
And this new realisation is her gift to herself
and her gift to the world.

An Unscripted Life

She's invited to be a part of a large gathering.
They've even asked her to speak and share
something.
She's agreed.

Standing up there, script in hand Maia's ready to
say what she thinks she wants to say.
That's how it has always been.
Put down your thoughts.
Perform as per the script. Be applauded for it.

A sudden gust of wind
and the piece of paper flew out of her hands.
Oh well, she sighs!
Then taking a deep and centering breath,
she allows herself to speak and say
what is naturally arising from within.

For the first time ever,
she feels completely free to express herself.
No script, no premeditated thoughts,
no one else's words.
This is all her own—her thoughts, her words,
being expressed by her.
And in that moment, she feels an immense sense

of liberation.
Even if for just a few minutes, she feels she has
been able to achieve something monumental.
Something she has been hoping to achieve
forever!

The response from the audience is mixed.
Some very loud claps and some no claps at all.
She smiles to herself.
The loud clappers will soon follow suit.
They sense and recognize what it means to be
'unshackled'.
And the non-clappers?
Oh well, breaking the shackles has never been
easy, has it?
Their time will come too.

The question remains, will Maia now be able to
break the shackles and live an unscripted life?

The Fight

Fighting for what she wanted had become the
norm.
She had begun to believe that was the only way
to get what was meant to be hers. . .

She's realising that if it was truly meant to be
hers, why did she need to fight for it?

Maybe what she was going after,
was never hers, to begin with?
Maybe those were never her battles to fight.

She's slowly beginning to step back.
Letting the Universe bring to her
what she asks for.
If she can get it from the Source,
Why would she want to rely on the human
middleman?

She's aiming to win the war.
She's choosing her battles.
Not every battle needs to be fought.

In fact, the fight has begun to leave her system.

And it feels so comforting,
to let the fight mode go.
And let life and breath
take its own sweet course.

Gaia's Arms

When you are tired
Rest your weary head on me

Unburden those shoulders
Of all that you've carried

Speak to me
Of all that hasn't dared leave your lips

Hug me
And let me hug you back

Let your eyes take in
The beauty meant for you

Become small
Without resenting it

Heal the wound
That's not yet healed

Feel the love
You've always longed for

Let the mother love you. Unconditionally.
She asks for nothing in return.

Rituals and Belonging

There was a time
when she followed rituals
because others told her to.
She did what others did.
And in doing so, she belonged, they said.
So she continued to practise.
And belong.

The same people broke her.
No one came along to find her.
Or heal her.
She wondered then,
where and to whom she belonged.

Rituals fell by the wayside.
Practices felt meaningless.
Not doing anything felt right.
In that state of doing nothing,
she began to experience a sense of belonging.
She realised she belonged but to herself.

Her practices and rituals took on a new flavour.

She practised silence.
Solitude became her friend.
Nature, her sanctuary.

Being in nature became her own sacred ritual.
Her altar was adorned not with idols and
religious symbols,
but with leaves, seeds, sticks, and rocks.

Having tasted her personal brand of rituals,
she no longer feels the need to go back and
belong.

She's found belongingness. In self.

Rain

Not realising when she had begun to cry,
she felt the tears fall onto her chest.
She let them fall.
The rain had done
what she hadn't been able to.
The dam broke.
She let the tears flow and cleanse her.

The healing was for the bigger things, and yet it
was the small things that broke her down.
That dear friend refusing to take her calls,
the grocery order getting cancelled,
the phone battery dying out just as she was
completing her email…

As she sat by the window,
the steady pitter-patter of the rain
began to calm her nerves.
When she thought back on it,
there was no one incident that came to mind.
And yet the agitation in her
had been building up over the past few days.

She kept her senses trained on the rain. Letting
the steady beat soothe her.

Tuning into nature's rhythms,
had always set right her own rhythm and energy.
It was no different now.

A small smile played on her lips,
just as the sun's rays fell on her desk.
Sunshine was never too far away.
It was at times just obscured by the clouds.

Cup O' Comfort

Every time she opens up a page to write,
either on the laptop or in her journal,
there is always a cup close at hand.
Tea or coffee, or even just some warm water
to soothe the throat, it really doesn't matter.
Writing and a cuppa always go together for her.

And even when she narrates an incident to a
friend or is on a video call, the cup is her
comfort,

just like a child holds on to a much used 'teddy'
or 'blankie'.

Sorting through her memories,
and the little notes that she has made
over the months and years,
the words begin to form in her head,
and the story begins to take shape.

She types furiously, stopping intermittently to
read and edit her writings if required,
all while reaching for the cup of comfort every
minute or so.
And if the cup is empty, she calls out to her
assistant for a refill.
She's too engrossed to get up and get it herself.

And there are those times when she is at a café,
allowing her thoughts to flow,
a pastry lying untouched, the cups of coffee
getting drained and refilled.
She pays no mind to the pastry,
it's the cup o' comfort that she seeks and needs
to be replenished.

She also has a circle of friends, her tribe as she
refers to them. When they meet, it's an absolute
riot over food, and multiple cups of tea, coffee
and the occasional vino.

Stories untold, stories re-told, made-up stories,
stories newly born. We are all just stories
waiting to be told, and she wants to tell them all.
All with a cup o' comfort in hand.

Being Luna

Being in tune with natural cycles had become her nature.

Being joyous and living days filled with activity during the full moon, allowing herself to slow down as the moon waned, and going deeper within during the dark moon, she felt aligned and one with all that was around her.

This particular dark moon, Maia asked her body what was it she needed.

There was no answer. Just silence. She again checked in with herself, "What is it that I need to know now?"

Nothing. Just silence came through. Taking that as her sign, she dropped everything, letting herself just be.

Keeping her pen and journal handy, she put

away her to-do list.
A couple of days of doing nothing
was what was calling out to her.

She stayed open to receiving signs.
Doing nothing, just staying open.
Breathing, relaxing completely and thoroughly
into the here and now, she let dreams flow.
Dreams brought her messages.
From time to time, she opened the journal and
penned down what wanted to come forth.
Not even glancing through the writing again,
she left that for later.

There were decisions to be made.
Not now, she told herself.
For now, let me listen to what the hidden moon
wants me to know.

Observation was her strength.
She allowed herself to be the sacred observer.
Watching as life unfolds, not engaging with it.
Being receptive to messages from the soul.
Keeping a keen ear out for messages from the
Universe.

She relaxed and turned languid as all the stored
tension of the last few days began to drain and
flow out of her.

Not wanting to hold on to any of it, letting Gaia
take it all in.
Every time she does this, she comes back fully
renewed to start the next cycle.

She also holds herself in anticipation, knowing
miracles can show up in the least expected ways.

Knowing everything will wait, and be there
when she returns, she allows her dreams to
incubate for the future, while she takes a deep,
long-awaited nap…

Savour The Moment

Just for today
With no promise of tomorrow
Explore the now
Live this moment

Flirt with it
Dance with it
Immerse yourself
Make love to this moment

When tomorrow comes
Live it all over again
And if it doesn't
You would have lived it anyway

On Comfort Zones

What purpose do comfort zones serve?
She used to feel they were there only to stop her
from moving ahead and achieving her goals.

But now she knows.
They are the pauses that come
between two stages of growth.
You cannot keep jet-setting
on the highway of life.
You need to be mindful that there are signals,
other people, vehicles…
And if you live in India, the odd cow, buffalo
and stray dog as well.
But I digress.

So, it was up to her
whether she wanted
to keep going at breakneck speed
or take pauses between speeding stints.

She chose the pauses.
There was growth happening.
And the growth needed to be
internalised and integrated.
And those newly acquired skills

needed to be used.
They had been learnt for a reason.

Or maybe the pause was even a stepping-stone
to get to the next level.
You cannot climb the entire flight of stairs in one
go if you are not used to it.
Your heart and body need the strength and
conditioning.
So, take those pauses as they come along. Rest
for a while.
Integrate and use the newly strengthened
muscle, and then move to the next level.

After all, even a sentence without commas and
full stops is just a bunch of words that make
little sense.

Music and Emotions

As they progressed on their road trip, he asked her to choose the music.
Plugging in her phone, Maia chose a playlist.

"You have quite an eclectic taste in music," he commented after a few numbers had played.
"What's your favourite genre?" he asked.

Giving him a raised eyebrow, "Do I really need to have one?
I just choose what matches my heartbeat in the moment, and play it," she said.

At his confused look, she placed her hand on his heart, searched the playlist,
and played something that happened to be one of his favourite tunes.
One which in fact he had written. But he did not tell her that. Just gave her a look out of the corner of his eye, and asked her why she chose that number.
"Because your heart seems to be beating a little faster than normal. And this will calm you down."

He smiled; little did she know he had written
this when he was in a confused state in his love
life.
And this had been almost a prayer seeking
guidance from the Gods of Love.
Cut to now, confused again at the emotions this
pint-sized being evoked in him, she had chosen
well for him, and he wondered how he would
convey these emotions to her.

Maybe write a song just for her?

Music truly was a universal language…

The Unhurried Life

In a culture that glorifies multi-tasking and
rewards over-achievement, how comforting it is
to do nothing.

Comforting?
Or does it make you oh-so-uncomfortable?
And what exactly is this discomfort about?
For not following societal norms, or for daring
to do what feels right to you?

Maia asked herself such questions from time to
time, letting the questions take root deep within
her psyche, and then allowing the answers to
grow as if they were sprouting forth like the
trunk and branches of a tree.
And if the tree could take its own sweet time
growing and bearing fruit, who was she to hurry
the process.

Letting the fruit ripen naturally only made it
sweeter.

And thus, she spent her days, slowly meandering
through life.

After all, as Lin Yutang says, if you can spend a perfectly useless afternoon in a perfectly useless manner, you have learned how to live.

Loneliness or Solitude

Loneliness brings sadness
Solitude brings peace

Loneliness wants
Solitude is complete in itself

Loneliness feels thrust upon you
Solitude is voluntary

Loneliness feels repulsive
Solitude is welcoming

Loneliness looks for distraction
Solitude stays with itself, within itself

Loneliness feels rejection
Solitude discovers hidden strengths

Loneliness flirts with the surface
Solitude romances depths unknown

What do you see it as? Can you change the
narrative? Shift the perspective?

Coffee. Croissant. And a Book.

It was her first time in a foreign land. Though she had been sent by the company on work, Maia had decided she would steal a few moments to be by herself and explore the city on her own. Being the diligent kind of a worker, she of course made sure her work and meetings did not suffer.

The weekend after she arrived, saw her sitting in a pretty little café on the pavement just outside her hotel. A black coffee, which she hated after only one sip, yet chose to finish because it seemed the right thing to do, a croissant, which she loved and promised herself she would have one of every day, and a book waiting to be opened, all lay on the table in front of her.

Her eyes wandered a little further to where a couple sat warming themselves in the morning sun, sharing a cigarette and laughing at some joke that only they were privy to.

Across the street, the flower seller was busy arranging the display of flowers to attract customers for the day. The reds, yellows and pinks all vied for attention, while the seller herself hiding behind her drab, old hat, coat, and scarf, paid loving attention to her gorgeous flowers.

Across the public square, the church bells announced the beginning of the Sunday mass, as a variety of church-goers dressed in their Sunday best, made their way in.

While not a religious person herself, she decided she would visit the church before she went back home later that week.

Finishing the last sip of the coffee with a grimace, and the last bite she had saved of the croissant, the book Maia decided could wait. The stories unfolding around her were much more absorbing.

On Creative Pursuits

Writer's block they say is real.
For some of us who like to write, we feel
blocked and stuck at times.
Like the words just refuse to come forth.

The same happens to my chef friend.
And to my artist friend.
And to my writer and poet friends too.

So, we have formed a clique.
Or as we like to call ourselves a 'coven'.
Go look it up if you don't know what a coven
means.

So, we witches decided a long time ago that we
wouldn't let artist's block bring us down. When
one of us experiences 'the block', the others
come along, and say, "Just do your thing.
Even if nothing comes to you; even if you feel

like the biggest imposter of all time, just bring forth your masterpiece (in progress).”

And then we have whatever the chef serves us, while listening to whatever the poet has penned down through the night.

One such day, the comedian brought her half-baked jokes. They were anything but funny. In fact, they were raw, just like the meat the chef had served at another such gathering. Eating something raw is hard. It’s difficult to digest. And yet we sat there, listening to the pain in her voice, at her attempts to be funny and make us laugh.

After we were done, the philosopher amongst us remarked, “The rawness of life is the raw material for our work. The world labels it as a creative pursuit. In all honesty, it is the wound that’s oozing out of us. All we do is embellish it with some beauty, and garnish it with some prettiness.”

What the connoisseur sees as art, is the artist’s pain, packaged as a masterpiece.

The Remedy

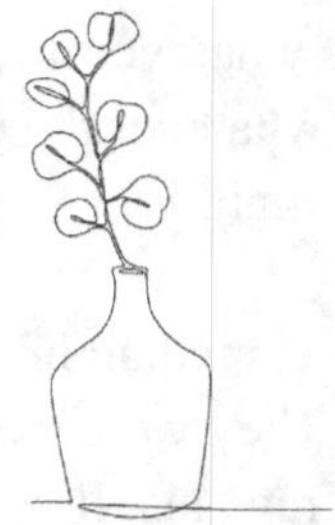

It arrives exactly when you need it.
You may not expect it, or even know that you
need it.
And yet it's there, just when you are ready to
give up.

Same was the case with me and stillness.
My soul yearned for it, while I kept up with a
steady stream of distractions.
And then things began to drop off, right out of
my orbit.
Wondering what I'd do with the extra time on
hand, I let myself be.

Oh, the discomfort of learning to just be. The
mind hankering to find something else to do.

The wardrobes got decluttered (multiple times,
mind you).

The kitchen was cleaned.

The shelves were organised to within an inch of
their lives.

I kept asking the emptiness I faced, "Who and
what are you?"
Till I was forced to answer that question myself.
And this is what I told the void, "You are exactly
what I'd thought you'd be."
"And what is that?" she asked.
"Dangerous to my mind, yet a remedy for my
soul."

And now? I know it's been good, and not just for
my soul.

For my body, heart, and mind as well...

Cleanse

The heart is calling for a wash
A cleanse and do-over
I am too vulnerable to do this alone
Sit with me
Hold my hand
Give me a hug
Don't ask. Don't say a word
Just be my mirror
When I feel cleansed
I'll let you know
And you can leave
And let me sleep the sleep of peace
That has been missing for days now
And when it's your turn to cleanse
Call upon me
I'll readily be your mirror too
For reflections of each other
Is all we are

On Being Disillusioned

She's allowing herself to be disillusioned from
time to time.
Life has been telling her that she can't have it
right every single time.
And she knows it's okay not to.

Putting herself through this almost feels like a
necessity.

The highs and lows are a part and parcel of life.
The lows come to make the highs feel better. But
staying in the highs isn't the thing to do or the
place to be.
Too many highs, and the lows feel harder to deal
with.
Balance is what she's striving to find.
It's all about balance.

A perfect heart never grows, because it has no
room to grow.
Let there be heartbreaks.

Experience pain.
Make room for the heart to grow.

Because when it begins to heal, is when the
heart begins to grow.

On Peace

The quiet of the hallowed temple halls
comforted her. The trees spoke to her.
The wind carried secrets only she could hear.
Warm hugs calmed her soul. The simple life
beckoned.

A cup of coffee sitting on the swing on the
balcony was the most precious part of her day.

These little things became her oasis in the midst
of a busy day.

She aimed to reach a stage where these became
the larger part of her day, with blips of busyness
interspersed.

She's getting there.
One hug, one sip of coffee, one word written,
slowly yet steadily she's getting there...

On Doing Nothing

She's happy with the place she now calls home. It's spacious. It's green. She has good people she calls neighbours. And yet she wakes up in the middle of the night reaching out to switch on the lamp that isn't there. The pillows and mattress still seem alien.

The traffic sounds different and less busy. The days are even less busy. She tries to fill them up with activity. She digs deep for the motivation that used to drive her. It comes but in spurts only. And then stalls like an engine asking for its oil to be replenished.

The words that used to easily come forth, are now barely there. Even writing, which she enjoys, now seems like a hard task.

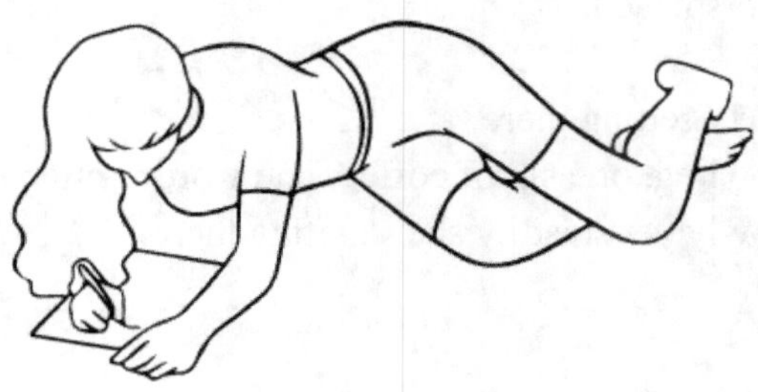

She sits on the swing relishing the sounds around her, watching the children play, the adults as they walk past her balcony, the pets frolicking on the grass. But all she really wants is to stay with the silence within her. The doing and noise have gotten too much. Even in their absence they still bother her. Doing nothing and saying nothing feels delicious. The silence is lusciously ripe. The nothingness full of potential.

She'll come back to exploring both. For now though, she wants none of it.

Borrowed Light

After retiring, he started the inn to stay busy. And he met many interesting folks here.

Maia was just another traveller who chose to stay at his inn.

While checking in, she left a bunch of books at the reception counter, saying anyone who wanted could take them. Recognizing her image on the back cover, curiosity got the better of him and he picked a copy. Back in his room, he couldn't stop reading. Completing the book, he was surprised to find tears running down his cheeks.

Late into the moonlit night, unable to sleep, he stood by the window. There she sat on the balcony, seemingly communing with the Moon. He stepped out, went, and sat next to her. Her cheeks were wet with tears too. "Why are you sad?" he asked.

She smiled through her tears. Not saying anything, she kept her gaze turned towards the skies.

"Celebrate your success. This is beautiful
writing," he said.

Maia smiled, "My fame will be gone someday.
Just as surely as the shine of the moon fades
every month. And I'll be shrouded in darkness
and oblivion, just as she (the moon) is."

Seemed like she'd forgotten her inner light. She
was living on borrowed light. And for now,
that's all she had chosen to share with the world.

Eye Of The Storm

The old has lost its power
The new is imminent, yet not quite here
In this waiting room of the present
Maia feels pulled back n' forth
Till her centre calls
In it, she rests
And what do you know?
She's become the eye of the storm
It rages on

While she watches
What calls to her
Is not on the surface

It's deep
Hidden under layers
Resting in the womb
Waiting to be birthed
She's the seed
She's the incubator
She's the midwife
She is also the newborn
While some write overheard stories
She knows this story is being self-written
Her every emotion flowing onto paper
One word and one feeling at a time

On Stepping Out

Choosing her own path had not come easily.
There were days she was terrified that she
would spend all her days alone. She could find
nothing even remotely attractive about living
alone. Till she realised otherwise.

The solitude began to talk to her. Comfort her.
She found solace in her own company. She
found she could live by herself.

She began to wander out of her self-imposed
exile into the neighbourhood. With tentative
smiles and hesitating words, she made a few
new friends and acquaintances. The fruit
vendor at the corner, the lady at the flower shop,
the barista at the coffee shop.

The quirky bookshop and its even quirkier
owner became her favourites. Losing herself in
the rows and rows of old books,

with many a suggestion from the helpful owner, she
discovered books that she had long forgotten.
And with it re-arose a love for words.

She'd pick a book once a week, read it, sell it
back, just because she could. And then pick
another one. This became a weekly ritual. The
conversation, suggestions for a suitable title,
choosing one, and taking it home with a big
smile.

The swing on the balcony, a cup of tea at hand,
and her read for the week.

Stepping out of her comfort zone had begun to
feel just a wee bit easier.

Metamorphosis

The balcony, sitting on the swing pen and paper or laptop in hand, dreaming, thinking,penning down thoughts had become Maia's new normal. Something that she enjoyed and looked forward to every day. Be it morning or evening, she made time for her musings and writings religiously.

The routine was set. However, what came out of her was constantly changing. Anger, regret, grief, blame; processing all the hurt and trauma, it would slowly change to indifference and then to acceptance, and even love, and beautiful words would flow.

Maia let it all pour forth onto her paper. As the seasons changed, her thoughts also kept shifting and changing. She loved every moment of it. Even when she hated what she was going through, she still loved it. She knew she was moving into her bigger life. She was leaving the smallness behind. She was constantly changing like the seasons. Growing, transforming into her most beautiful self yet.

The butterfly that she saw flitting about had also
gone through similar changes, without
complaint. The Divine was guiding her through
it all. Who was she to even complain, when
she knew she was just a part of the Divine plan
unfolding in good time and at the right pace?

The Insight

She's had an insight about why she wants to keep doing something. She's been feeling insignificant and unseen. While her soul is happy with the do-nothing, her ego is not.

And this is why she keeps wanting to even go out to social events, post on social media, and continue with meaningless work.

The ego craves recognition, accolades, and being seen.

While the soul says, forget it. Just live your life. The world doesn't need to know what you are doing. Staying relevant or disappearing into oblivion for a while, what is it going to be?

On Depression

Maia woke up a little upset. Things were on her mind and had been pulling her down. She asked herself, 'Am I depressed?' Leaving the question to marinate in the juices of her mind, she went about her day.

Groceries were ordered, payments were made, instructions were issued to the staff, and hugs given to loved ones. Nothing seemed to lift the pall hanging over her head. Over her lunch salad, she again asked herself, "Depressed, am I?" Leaving it for a second marination, she turned to binge-watch her current favourite show.

She was tempted to phone a friend to see if she could hash this out. Knowing the friend was

busy at work, she let it be, choosing instead to
let the mind do its thing. Being a good cook,
she knew, the longer the marination, the juicier
the dish, or in this case the answers, would turn
out to be.

With her evening cup of masala chai in hand,
she picked up her laptop to go sit on her
favourite swing and type out and see what
wanted to come forth. The tea seemed tasteless
to the palate. Going into the kitchen she saw
some ripe, juicy peaches sitting on the counter,
asking to be devoured.

Peach in hand, laptop on the… well, lap, she
furiously typed all that had been marinating in
her for so long. As the words poured out of her,
she realised there were two things that
could always get her out of her funk. Words and
fruit. Words helped sort through thoughts,
and fruit? Fruit brought forth her happy feelings.
And added to the juiciness of the writing.

And just like that, out went the funk!!!

Getting up to play some peppy tunes, she asked
once more, "Depression? What's that???"

On Deep Rest

She feels a need to rest. Deep rest is what her
soul is seeking. Like letting go of even holding
up a finger. No burden, no thought, no mind.
Just sinking into the bosom of Mother Earth.

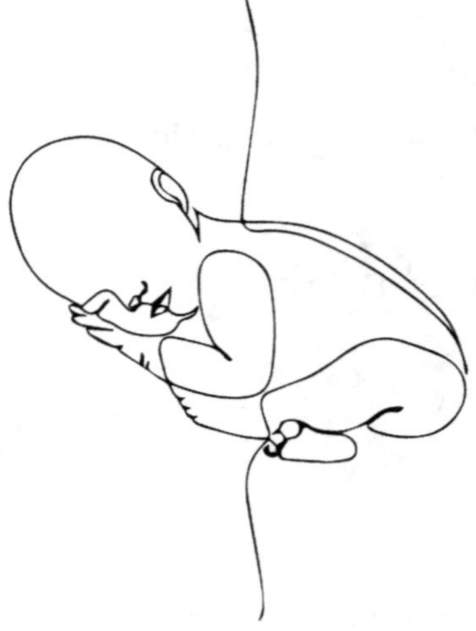

Let Pachamama take her in her arms and hold
her. Comforting her and nourishing her.
Replenish is the word that comes to her mind
right now. And what better place to renew
and replenish than at her Divine mother's
bosom?

The Shift

There is a need to pause, to drop all the doing.
Or maybe life's just asking me to slow down.
It's what I've always wanted to do while being in
the midst of all the noise. And now when
it's happening, it's just beginning to feel so alien.
And lonely.

Is this what a personal transition feels like?

Shedding the old, and emerging into the new are
states we hear about. The in-between or the
liminal period is what no one speaks of. Now I
know why they don't. No words can really
describe what this feeling is.

Just stay with it. With these alien feelings.
The shift will occur even without you knowing
it's happening.

The Golden Hour

The sun setting on the horizon
A sense of helplessness
Like I have no control over what's happening
This sense of loneliness and longing
That nighttime brings with it

Those feelings still exist
Yet today feels a wee bit different
As if it isn't going to be that sad after all
A tiny kernel of hope
Seems to be present in me today

Where is it coming from, I ask
Is it the time of day?
The golden hue surrounding us
Making everything seem magical and surreal

Maybe it's the idyllic rustic surroundings
Or the tunes playing
As if the playlist senses
What it is I am feeling and wanting more of

What is it?
The golden hour?
The company?
The magical tunes?
A shift that I'm sensing.
Moving into the new?
The knowing that all is well.

Living it feels magical
Questioning it seems futile
So why question it at all?
Let me just live it

Be, and It Is

She's waited in anticipation.
She's lain awake for way too long now.
Realisation has been slow to come.
But it has finally arrived.

Shedding those layers.
Dropping the excess.
Paring herself down
to only what feels essential

She's now ready.
Ready to live
the authentic life
she was always meant for.

Asking what to leave and what to take,
the answer is always,
'Take only so much that you can carry'.
The rest is not meant for you.
More will show up when you need it.

For now, with a heart full of gratitude
and feet waiting to traverse
the next steps of this precious journey,
Her eyes are eager to witness new horizons.
Fear shows up.

The old and the familiar call her back.
But she knows.
In fact, she's known this for a long time now.

It's time.

And nothing and no one can stop
this tide from turning,
this flower from blooming
and this story from unfolding.

Spreading her wings,
she's taking to the skies for lands unknown,
for shores even more beautiful
than the ones she's lived on.

When she's confused
and unable to imagine what it'll be like
The words of a wise one come to remind her
BE, and IT IS...

Making Connections

It was a bright, pleasant day. Seeing the two old
ladies clicking pictures of one another, she
offered, "Would you like me to take a picture of
you both?"

After only a brief hesitation, one of the cute
oldies agreed. So she asked them to pose by
the flowers, and clicked a few pictures for them.
Handing their phone back, she was about
to walk away, when one of them hesitatingly
asked me, "You want me to 'make picture' for
you?" Not having expected it, she was pleasantly
surprised, and decided to take them up on
the offer.

She stood patiently, while the cute lady figured
out how to click pics on a phone different than
her own.

An elderly gentleman passing by seemed to have
been watching this whole scenario unfold.
He stood behind the lady and peeped into the
phone's camera as she clicked. And then he
looked up at Maia, winked, and with his fingers
signed that it was a good click. Maia burst
into laughter at this whole drama unfolding. And
the lady caught her laughing on camera.

And what a happy picture it turned out to be!!
As happy as the entire encounter was.

Why do we hesitate to ask others for these small
little favours? It can be a mutual favour, or
maybe not. It's okay to smile at a stranger, offer
to or ask someone to click a picture, share a
laugh with someone even.

Just makes for some happy moments in this
journey called life.

On Mindfulness

When I chose to live mindfully...
The world, it just seemed a little brighter
The smile, it felt a wee bit happier
The people, they were a lot friendlier
And life? Life just seemed a lot more liveable